THIS J

BELONGS TO

DIA PRINT LAB

diaprintlab@gmail.com

66320495R00074

Made in the USA
Columbia, SC
16 July 2019